CW00552744

SOCCER

THE INTERNATIONAL LINE-UPS & STATISTICS SERIES –

ECUADOR 1938-1997

STATISTICS
Gustavo Ramirez Benavides

EDITOR
Michael Robinson

Price
£5.95

CONTENTS

About the Author..3

Ecuador Full International Matches 1938-1997........................... 4-44

British Library Cataloguing in Publication Data
A catalogue record for this book is available from the British Library
ISBN 1-86223-016-1

Copyright © 1997; SOCCER BOOKS LIMITED (01472-696226)
72, St. Peters' Avenue, Cleethorpes, N.E. Lincolnshire, DN35 8HU, England

Printed by Joshua Horgan Print Partnership, 246 Marston Road, Oxford, OX3 0EL

THE AUTHOR

Gustavo Ramirez Benavides was born in El Guabo, Ecuador, on the 16th December 1964.

An architect, his main interest is the collection of books, postcards and photos of stadia around the world.

In 1991, Soccer Book Publishing Limited published his book: 'Football in Ecuador – The Grounds & History' and he has contributed articles to 'Spaziosport' (Italy) and 'Groundtastic' (England). He has also printed more than 130 postcards of stadia and is preparing an updated book on Ecuadorian stadia.

1: 11th August 1938
v PERU *Bogota*
F. Martinez Roiz
E. Ronquillo
L. Hungria
Sandoval
A. Zambrano
J.M. Vasconez
E. Alvarez
A. Suarez
M. Arenas
E. Herrera
C.A. Freire
Result 1-9 A. Suarez

2: 15th August 1938
v VENEZUELA *Bogota*
H. Vasquez
L. Hungria
E. Ronquillo
Jabs
J.M. Vasconez
A. Zambrano
Sola
C.A. Freire
E. Herrera
A. Suarez
E. Alvarez
Result 5-2 A. Suarez, M. Arenas, E. Herrera, C.A. Freire, Castillo (own goal)

3: 18th August 1938
v BOLIVIA *Bogota*
F. Martinez Roiz
J. Naranjo
E. Ronquillo
Sola
A. Zambrano
J.M. Vasconez
A. Suarez
Abril
E. Herrera
Lopez
C.A. Freire
Result 1-1 E. Herrera

4: 21st August 1938
v COLOMBIA *Bogota*
F. Martinez Roiz
E. Ronquillo
L. Hungria
Sola
M. Arenas
A. Zambrano
J.M. Vasconez
A. Suarez
Abril
E. Herrera
Lopez
C.A. Freire
Result 2-1 E. Herrera, C.A. Freire

5: 22nd August 1938
v BOLIVIA *Bogota*
F. Martinez Roiz
E. Ronquillo
L. Hungria
Sola
A. Zambrano
J.M. Vasconez
A. Suarez
Abril
E. Herrera
Lopez
C.A. Freire
Result 1-2 A. Zambrano

6: 15th January 1939
v PERU *Lima*
H. Vasquez
E. Ronquillo
A. Solis
J. Merino
A. Zambrano (sub J. Peralta)
E. Arias (sub J.M. Vasconez)
E. Cevallos
R. Unamuno (sub M. Alcivar)
E. Herrera
A. Suarez
C.A. Freire
Result 2-5 M. Alcivar, A. Suarez

7: 22nd January 1939
v URUGUAY *Lima*
H. Vasquez
E. Ronquillo
A. Solis
J.M. Vasconez
J. Peralta
J. Merino
L. Elizalde
E. Herrera
M. Alcivar
M. Arenas (sub A. Suarez)
E. Cevallos
Result 0-6

10: 2nd February 1941
v CHILE *Santiago*
I. Molina
L. Hungria
J. Laurido
J. Merino
A. Romo
L.A. Mendoza
A. Suarez
E. Raymondi
M. Alcivar
E. Cevallos
C.A. Freire
Result 0-5

8: 5th February 1939
v CHILE *Lima*
F. Martinez Roiz
L. Hungria
E. Ronquillo
E. Cevallos
J. Peralta
J.M. Vasconez
A. Suarez
M. Alcivar
M. Arenas
J. Laurido (sub F. Bohorquez)
C.A. Freire
Result 1-4 M. Arenas

11: 9th February 1941
v URUGUAY *Santiago*
I. Molina
J. Laurido
L. Hungria
L.A. Mendoza
J. Peralta
V. Aguirre
E. Cevallos
A. Suarez
E. Raymondi
M. Alcivar
C.A. Freire
Result 0-6

9: 12th February 1939
v PARAGUAY *Lima*
H. Vasquez
E. Ronquillo
A. Solis
E. Arias
J. Peralta
J.M. Vasconez
E. Cevallos
M. Alcivar (sub A. Suarez)
M. Arenas
E. Herrera
C.A. Freire
Result 1-3 M. Arenas

12: 16th February 1941
v ARGENTINA *Santiago*
H. Santoliva (sub I. Molina)
J. Laurido
L. Hungria (sub C. Angulo)
C. Garnica
J. Peralta
L.A. Mendoza
E. Cevallos
A. Suarez
E. Raymondi (sub E. Stacey)
M. Alcivar
C.A. Freire
Result 1-6 C.A. Freire

13: 23rd February 1941
v PERU *Santiago*
I. Molina
C. Angulo
J. Laurido
J. Merino
J. Peralta
L.A. Mendoza
E. Cevallos
A. Suarez
M. Alcivar
E. Herrera
C.A. Freire
Result 0-4

14: 18th January 1942
v URUGUAY *Montevideo*
A.N. Medina (sub H. Vasquez)
L. Hungria
E. Ronquillo
J. Merino (sub Sempertegui)
A. Zambrano
L.A. Mendoza
E. Alvarez
J.M. Jimenez
M. Alcivar
E. Herrera
P. Acevedo
Result 0-7

15: 22nd January 1942
v ARGENTINA *Montevideo*
A.N. Medina
E. Ronquillo
F.L. Zurita
Sempertegui (sub C. Torres)
A. Zambrano
L.A. Mendoza
E. Alvarez
J.M. Jimenez
M. Alcivar
G.H. Gavilanez
P. Acevedo
Result 0-12

16: 25th January 1942
v PARAGUAY *Montevideo*
A.N. Medina
L. Hungria (sub F.L. Zurita)
E. Ronquillo
C. Torres
A. Zambrano
L.A. Mendoza
E. Alvarez
Abril (sub E. Herrera)
M. Alcivar
J.M. Jimenez
P. Acevedo
Result 1-3 E. Herrera

17: 28th January 1942
v PERU *Montevideo*
A.N. Medina
L. Hungria
F.L. Zurita
C. Torres
A. Zambrano
L.A. Mendoza (sub Medina)
E. Alvarez
J.M. Jimenez
M. Alcivar
G.H. Gavilanez (sub E. Herrera)
P. Acevedo
Result 1-2 J.M. Jimenez

18: 31st January 1942
v BRAZIL *Montevideo*
A.N. Medina
L. Hungria
E. Ronquillo
J. Merino
A. Zambrano
L.A. Mendoza
E. Alvarez
J.M. Jimenez
M. Alcivar (sub C. Torres)
E. Herrera
P. Acevedo
Result 1-5 E. Alvarez

19: 5th February 1942
v CHILE *Montevideo*
A.N. Medina
L. Hungria
E. Ronquillo (sub F.L. Zurita)
C. Torres
A. Zambrano
L.A. Mendoza
E. Alvarez
J.M. Jimenez (sub M. Alcivar)
G.H. Gavilanez
J.L. Mendoza
P. Acevedo
Result 1-2 M. Alcivar

20: 14th January 1945
v CHILE *Santiago*
A.N. Medina
Villagomez
F.L. Zurita
L.A. Mendoza
E. Alvarez
Mejia
J.L. Mendoza
J.M. Jimenez
E. Raymondi
V. Aguayo
P. Acevedo
Result 3-6 E. Raymondi 2, Mendoza

21: 24th January 1945
v URUGUAY *Santiago*
A.N. Medina
J. Henriquez
F.L. Zurita
L.A. Mendoza
E. Alvarez
Mejia
J.L. Mendoza
J.M. Jimenez
E. Raymondi (sub Albornoz)
V. Aguayo
P. Acevedo
Result 1-5 V. Aguayo

22: 31st January 1945
v ARGENTINA *Santiago*
A.N. Medina
F.L. Zurita (sub Villagomez)
J. Henriquez
L.A. Mendoza
E. Alvarez
Mejia
J.L. Mendoza
J.M. Jimenez
E. Raymondi
V. Aguayo
P. Acevedo
Result 2-4 V. Aguayo, J.L. Mendoza

23: 11th February 1945
v BOLIVIA *Santiago*
A.N. Medina
J. Henriquez
F.L. Zurita
L.A. Mendoza (sub C. Garnica)
E. Alvarez
Mejia
J.L. Mendoza (sub Montenegro)
J.M. Jimenez
E. Raymondi
V. Aguayo
P. Acevedo
Result 0-0

24: 18th February 1945
v COLOMBIA *Santiago*
A.N. Medina
J. Henriquez
F.L. Zurita (sub Villagomez)
E. Alvarez
C. Garnica
Mejia
Montenegro
J.M. Jimenez
E. Raymondi
V. Aguayo
P. Acevedo (sub J.L. Mendoza)
Result 1-3 V. Aguayo

25: 21st February 1945
v BRAZIL *Santiago*
A.N. Medina (sub Suarez)
F.L. Zurita
J. Henriquez (sub Villagomez)
L.A. Mendoza
E. Alvarez
Mejia
Montenegro
J.M. Jimenez
Albornoz
V. Aguayo
J.L. Mendoza
Result 2-9 V. Aguayo, Albornoz

26: 30th November 1947
v BOLIVIA *Guayaquil*
A.N. Medina
J. Henriquez
F.L. Zurita
C. Torres
E. Alvarez (sub E. Ortiz)
J.L. Mendoza
L.A. Mendoza
J.M. Jimenez
F. Zenck
V. Aguayo (sub E. Cantos)
G. Pozo
Result 2-2 J.M. Jimenez 2

27: 4th December 1947
v COLOMBIA *Guayaquil*
L.A. Carrillo
J. Henriquez
F.L. Zurita
H. Marin
E. Ortiz
A.R. Riveros
V. Cevallos
C. Garnica
J.M. Jimenez
E. Cantos
G. Pozo
Result 0-0

28: 11th December 1947
v CHILE *Guayaquil*
L.A. Carrillo
C. Sanchez
F.L. Zurita
A. Molina
E. Alvarez
H. Marin
V. Cevallos
J.M. Jimenez
F. Zenck
G. Pozo
J. Vargas (sub V. Aguayo)
Result 0-3

29: 16th December 1947
v URUGUAY *Guayaquil*
L.A. Carrillo
J. Henriquez
C. Sanchez
C. Torres
E. Ortiz
J.L. Mendoza (sub J.M. Jimenez)
L.A. Mendoza
C. Garnica
G.H. Gavilanez
V. Aguayo
G. Pozo
Result 1-6 C. Garnica

30: 20th December 1947
v PERU *Guayaquil*
L.A. Carrillo
J. Henriquez
C. Sanchez
C. Torres
E. Ortiz
J.L. Mendoza
J.M. Jimenez
L.A. Mendoza
C. Garnica
V. Aguayo
G. Pozo
Result 0-0

8

31: 25th December 1947
v ARGENTINA *Guayaquil*
A.N. Medina
J. Henriquez
F.L. Zurita
A.R. Riveros
E. Alvarez (sub E. Ortiz)
L.A. Mendoza
V. Cevallos
J.M. Jimenez
F. Zenck (sub G.H. Gavilanez)
V. Aguayo
G. Pozo
Result 0-2

32: 29th December 1947
v PARAGUAY *Guayaquil*
L.A. Carrillo
C. Sanchez
F.L. Zurita
A. Molina
E. Alvarez
H. Marin
V. Cevallos
J.M. Jimenez
C. Garnica
E. Cantos (sub J. Vargas)
G. Pozo
Result 0-4

33: 3rd April 1949
v BRAZIL *Rio De Janeiro*
F. Torres (sub L.A. Carrillo)
C. Sanchez
Bermeo
Salgado
Vasquez
H. Marin
V. Arteaga
E. Cantos
S. Chuchuca
J. Vargas
G. Pozo (sub R. Maldonado)
Result 1-9 S. Chuchuca

34: 10th April 1949
v PARAGUAY *Rio De Janeiro*
F. Torres
C. Sanchez
Bermeo
Salgado
Vasquez
H. Marin
V. Arteaga
E. Cantos
R. Maldonado
J. Vargas
G. Pozo
Result 0-1

35: 13th April 1949
v URUGUAY *Rio De Janeiro*
F. Torres
C. Sanchez
Bermeo
Vasquez
H. Marin
Salgado
V. Arteaga
E. Cantos (sub S. Chuchuca)
R. Maldonado
J. Vargas
G. Pozo
Result 2-3 V. Arteaga, J. Vargas

36: 17th April 1949
v CHILE *Rio De Janeiro*
F. Torres
C. Sanchez
Bermeo
Salgado
Vasquez
H. Marin
V. Arteaga
S. Chuchuca
R. Maldonado
J. Vargas
G. Pozo
Result 0-1

37: 20th April 1949
v PERU *Rio De Janeiro*
L.A. Carrillo (sub F. Torres)
C. Sanchez
Bermeo
Salgado
H. Marin
J.M. Jimenez
J. Vargas
E. Cantos
S. Chuchuca
R. Maldonado
G. Pozo
Result 0-4

38: 25th April 1949
v BOLIVIA *Sao Paulo*
F. Torres
C. Sanchez
Bermeo
Andrade
E. Cantos
H. Marin
V. Arteaga
M. Spencer (sub J.M. Jimenez)
S. Chuchuca
J. Vargas
G. Pozo
Result 0-2

39: 3rd May 1949
v COLOMBIA *Rio De Janeiro*
F. Torres
C. Sanchez
Bermeo
A.R. Riveros
J. Cantos
Salgado
V. Arteaga (sub M. Spencer)
E. Cantos (sub C. Garnica)
R. Maldonado
J. Vargas
G. Andrade
Result 4-1 J. Cantos, J. Vargas, G. Andrade, R. Maldonado

40: 28th February 1953
v PERU *Lima*
A. Bonnard
C. Sanchez
J. Henriquez
H. Marin (sub C. Solorzano)
J. Izaguirre
A.R. Riveros
V. Arteaga
D. Pinto
S. Chuchuca (sub Maranon)
J. Vargas
E. Guzman
Result 0-1

41: 4th March 1953
v PARAGUAY *Lima*
A. Bonnard
C. Sanchez
J. Henriquez
H. Marin
J. Izaguirre
A.R. Riveros
J.V. Balseca
D. Pinto
Maranon
J. Vargas
R.P. de la Torre (sub E. Guzman)
Result 0-0

42: 8th March 1953
v BOLIVIA *Lima*
A. Bonnard
C. Sanchez
J. Henriquez
H. Marin
J. Izaguirre
A.R. Riveros
J.V. Balseca
D. Pinto (sub V. Arteaga)
Maranon
R. Maldonado (sub J. Vargas)
E. Guzman
Result 1-1 E. Guzman

43: 12th March 1953
v BRAZIL *Lima*
A. Bonnard
C. Sanchez
J. Henriquez
C. Solorzano
J. Izaguirre
A.R. Riveros (sub G. Solis)
J.V. Balseca
D. Pinto
S. Chuchuca
J. Vargas
E. Guzman
Result 0-2

44: 19th March 1953
v CHILE *Lima*
A. Bonnard
C. Sanchez
J. Henriquez
M. Lovato (sub A.R. Riveros)
H. Marin
G. Solis
J.V. Balseca
D. Pinto
S. Chuchuca (sub Maranon)
J. Vargas
E. Guzman
Result 0-3

45: 23rd March 1953
v URUGUAY *Lima*
A. Bonnard
C. Sanchez
J. Henriquez
C. Solorzano (sub M. Lovato)
J. Izaguirre
A.R. Riveros (sub G. Solis)
J.V. Balseca
D. Pinto
S. Chuchuca (sub V. Arteaga)
J. Vargas
E. Guzman
Result 0-6

46: 27th February 1955
v CHILE *Santiago*
A. Bonnard
C. Sanchez
O. Zambrano (sub C. Valencia)
C. Alume
J. Izaguirre (sub W. Villacreses)
G. Gando
J.V. Balseca
E. Cantos (sub D. Pinto)
I. Matute
C. Merizalde
C. Canarte
Result 1-7 W. Villacreses

47: 9th March 1955
v ARGENTINA *Santiago*
A. Bonnard
C. Sanchez
H. Gonzabay
C. Valencia
G. Solis
M. Saeteros (sub D. Pinto)
J.V. Balseca
W. Villacreses
I. Matute
C. Merizalde
E. Cantos (sub C. Canarte)
Result 0-4

48: 13th March 1955
v PERU *Santiago*
A. Bonnard
C. Sanchez
C. Valencia
W. Villacreses
G. Solis
H. Gonzabay
M. Saeteros
D. Pinto
J.V. Balseca
I. Matute
E. Trivino
Result 2-4 I. Matute 2

49: 16th March 1955
v PARAGUAY *Santiago*
A. Bonnard
C. Sanchez
C. Valencia
H. Gonzabay
W. Villacreses
G. Solis
M. Saeteros
C. Merizalde
I. Matute
J.V. Balseca
E. Trivino
Result 0-2

50: 23rd March 1955
v URUGUAY *Santiago*
A. Bonnard (sub H. Mejia)
C. Sanchez
G. Solis
H. Gonzabay
J. Izaguirre (sub G. Gando)
W. Villacreses (sub R. Gomez)
M. Saeteros
I. Matute
J.V. Balseca
C. Merizalde
C. Canarte
Result 1-5 I. Matute

51: 7th March 1957
v URUGUAY *Lima*
C. Yu-Lee
R. Arguello (sub E. Martinez)
H. Gonzabay
L. Macias
C. Solorzano (sub J. Galarza)
J. Caisaguano
G. Salcedo
E. Cantos
J. Larraz
J. Vargas (sub C. Merizalde)
C. Canarte
Result 2-5 E. Cantos, J. Larraz

52: 10th March 1957
v PERU *Lima*
A. Bonnard
R. Arguello
C. Solorzano (sub J. Caisaguano)
C. Sanchez
J. Galarza
H. Gonzabay
J.V. Balseca
E. Cantos (sub G. Salcedo)
I. Matute (sub J. Vargas)
J. Larraz
C. Canarte
Result 1-2 E. Cantos

53: 17th March 1957
v ARGENTINA *Lima*
A. Bonnard
R. Arguello
J. Caisaguano (sub H. Pardo)
L. Marcias
C. Solorzano
H. Gonzabay
G. Salcedo
D. Pinto (sub I. Matute)
J.V. Balseca
J. Larraz
J. Miranda
Result 0-3

54: 21st March 1957
v BRAZIL *Lima*
A. Bonnard (sub C. Yu-Lee)
R. Arguello
H. Gonzabay
L. Macias
J. Caisaguano (sub H. Pardo)
C. Solorzano
J.V. Balseca
E. Cantos
J. Larraz
J. Vargas
C. Canarte
Result 1-7 J. Larraz (pen)

55: 24th March 1957
v CHILE *Lima*
A. Bonnard
H. Pardo
C. Solorzano
R. Arguello
J. Vargas
C. Sanchez
G. Salcedo (sub C. Canarte)
E. Cantos (sub I. Matute)
J.V. Balseca
J. Larraz
J. Miranda
Result 2-2 J. Larraz (pen), E. Cantos

56: 1st April 1957
v COLOMBIA *Lima*
A. Bonnard
H. Pardo
C. Sanchez
R. Arguello
C. Solorzano (sub R. Gomez)
J. Vargas
G. Salcedo
E. Cantos (sub D. Pinto)
J.V. Balseca (sub I. Matute)
J. Larraz
J. Miranda
Result 1-4 J. Larraz

57: 6th December 1959
v URUGUAY *Guayaquil*
A. Bonnard
R. Arguello
H. Gonzabay
F. Nall (sub J. Izaguirre)
R. Gomez
J. Galarza (sub R. Reeves Patterson)
J.V. Balseca
A. Spencer
C. Raffo
L. Palacios
F. Almeida
Result 0-4

58: 12th December 1959
v ARGENTINA *Guayaquil*
A. Bonnard
R. Arguello
H. Gonzabay
J. Izaguirre
J. Galarza (sub R. Reeves Patterson)
R. Gomez
J.V. Balseca
L. Palacios
C. Raffo (sub M. Saeteros)
A. Spencer
C. Canarte (sub F. Almeida)
Result 1-1 C. Raffo

59: 19th December 1959
v BRAZIL *Guayaquil*
A. Bonnard
R. Arguello
H. Gonzabay
J. Izaguirre
R. Gomez
J. Galarza (sub R. Reeves Patterson)
J.V. Balseca (sub N. Aurea)
L. Palacios
C. Raffo
A. Spencer
C. Canarte
Result 1-3 C. Raffo

60: 25th December 1959
v PARAGUAY *Guayaquil*
C. Yu-Lee
R. Arguello
H. Gonzabay
F. Nall
R. Gomez
J. Galarza
J.V. Balseca
L. Palacios (sub E. Guerra)
C. Raffo
A. Spencer (sub M. Saeteros)
C. Canarte
Result 3-1 A. Spencer, J.V. Balseca, C. Canarte

61: 27th December 1959
v BRAZIL *Guayaquil*
C. Yu-Lee
R. Arguello
V. Lecaro
F. Nall (sub J. Ubilla)
R. Reeves Patterson (sub Cruz)
J. Galarza (sub R. Gomez)
J.V. Balseca
L. Palacios
M. Saeteros
C. Raffo
C. Canarte
Result 1-2 C. Raffo

62: 4th December 1961
v ARGENTINA *Guayaquil*
C. Yu-Lee
J. Izaguirre
V. Lecaro
L. Macias
R. Gomez
J. Galarza
J.V. Balseca
A. Spencer
C. Raffo
J. Bolanos
C. Canarte
Result 3-6 A. Spencer, C. Raffo 2

63: 17th December 1961
v ARGENTINA *Buenos Aires*
C. Yu-Lee
V. Lecaro
J. Izaguirre
L. Macias
R. Gomez
J. Galarza
J.V. Balseca
L. Palacios
C. Raffo
J. Bolanos
C. Canarte
Result 0-5

64: 10th March 1963
v BOLIVIA *La Paz*
E. Mejia
A. Quijano
V. Lecaro
J. Galarza
L. Macias
R. Reeves Patterson
J. Bolanos
J.V. Balseca
C. Raffo
Raymondi
T. Larrea
Result 4-4 C. Raffo 2, Raymondi, J. Bolanos

65: 14th March 1963
v PARAGUAY *La Paz*
E. Mejia (sub Ansaldo)
A. Quijano
V. Lecaro
J. Galarza
L. Macias
C. Pineda
J. Bolanos
G. Gando
C. Raffo
Raymondi
T. Larrea
Result 1-3 C. Raffo

66: 17th March 1963
v PERU *La Paz*
Ansaldo (sub E. Mejia)
A. Quijano
L. Macias
V. Lecaro (sub M. Bustamante)
Johnson
R. Reeves Patterson
J. Bolanos
G. Gando
C. Raffo
Raymondi (sub Azon)
T. Larrea
Result 1-2 C. Raffo

67: 20th March 1963
v ARGENTINA *Cochabamba*
E. Mejia
Johnson
M. Bustamante
V. Lecaro
L. Macias
C. Pineda
J. Bolanos
G. Gando (sub L. Palacios)
C. Raffo
Raymondi
T. Larrea
Result 2-4 C. Pineda, L. Palacios

68: 27th March 1963
v BRAZIL *Cochabamba*
E. Mejia
A. Quijano (sub L. Macias)
R. Reeves Patterson
V. Lecaro
M. Bustamante
Johnson (sub J. Galarza)
Azon
G. Gando
B. Merizalde (sub C. Raffo)
L. Palacios
T. Larrea
Result 2-2 C. Raffo, G. Gando

69: 31st March 1963
v COLOMBIA *La Paz*
E. Mejia
Johnson
V. Lecaro
L. Macias
M. Bustamante
C. Pineda
J. Bolanos
G. Gando
Raymondi
C. Raffo
T. Larrea
Result 4-3 C. Raffo 2, Raymondi, J. Bolanos

70: 20th July 1965
v COLOMBIA *Barranquilla*
Ansaldo
A. Quijano
V. Lecaro
L. Macias
M. Bustamante
R. Gomez
C. Canarte
W. Munoz
J. Bolanos
Raymondi
T. Larrea
Result 1-0 W. Munoz

71: 25th July 1965
v COLOMBIA *Guayaquil*
Ansaldo
A. Quijano
V. Lecaro
L. Macias
M. Bustamante
R. Gomez
Zambrano
W. Munoz
J. Bolanos
Raymondi
T. Larrez
Result 2-0 Raymondi 2

72: 15th August 1965
v CHILE *Guayaquil*
Ansaldo
A. Quijano
V. Lecaro
L. Macias
M. Bustamante
R. Gomez
C. Canarte
W. Munoz
J. Bolanos
A. Spencer
Raymondi
Result 2-2 A. Spencer, Raymondi

15

73: 22nd August 1965
v CHILE *Santiago*
A. Bonnard
A. Quijano
V. Lecaro
L. Macias
F. Mina
Zambrano
C. Canarte
W. Munoz
J. Bolanos
A. Spencer
T. Larrea
Result 1-3 A. Spencer

74: 12th October 1965
v CHILE *Lima*
Helio Carreira Da Silva "Helinho"
A. Quijano
V. Lecaro
L. Macias
F. Mina
C. Pineda
R. Gomez
W. Munoz
J. Bolanos
A. Spencer
B. Merizalde
Result 1-2 L. Macias

75: 21st December 1966
v PARAGUAY *Guayaquil*
Helinho
A. Quijano
V. Lecaro
L. Macias
M. Bustamante
J. Bolanos
C. Pineda
W. Munoz (sub J. Delgado Mana)
F. Lasso (sub B. Merizalde)
P. Carrera
C. Canarte
Result 2-2 P. Carrera, W. Munoz

76: 28th December 1966
v PARAGUAY *Asuncion*
Helinho
A. Quijano
V. Lecaro
L. Macias
M. Bustamante
J. Bolanos
H. Morales (sub E. Portilla)
W. Munoz
F. Lasso
P. Carrera (sub T. Rodriguez)
C. Canarte
Result 1-3 W. Munoz

77: 22nd June 1969
v COLOMBIA *Guayaquil*
Maldonado
A. Quijano
E. Portilla
Quintero
L. Macias
Cardenas
J. Bolanos (sub Contreras)
Rangel (sub W. Munoz)
J. Tapia
F. Lasso (sub Malagon)
Espinoza
Result 4-1 F. Lasso 2, W. Munoz 2

78: 6th July 1969
v URUGUAY *Guayaquil*
M. Ordenana
A. Quijano
E. Portilla
Quintero
R. Tobar
Cardenas
J. Tapia
W. Munoz
F. Lasso (sub T. Rodriguez)
J. Bolanos
Espinoza (sub Rangel)
Result 0-2

16

79: 20th July 1969
v URUGUAY *Montevideo*
Maldonado
V. Lecaro
L. Macias
A. Quijano
Quintero
R. Tobar
W. Munoz
Noriega
J. Tapia (sub T. Rodriguez)
J. Bolanos
Espinoza (sub Malagon)
Result 0-1

80: 27th July 1969
v CHILE *Santiago*
Maldonado
Echanique
E. Portilla
L. Macias
R. Tobar
Quintero
Noriega
J. Tapia (sub Cardenas)
W. Munoz
F. Lasso
J. Bolanos
Result 1-4 L. Macias

81: 3rd August 1969
v CHILE *Guayaquil*
Maldonado
A. Quijano
V. Lecaro
L. Macias
R. Tobar
Noriega
J. Tapia (sub F. Lasso)
W. Munoz
J. Bolanos
T. Rodriguez (sub Malagon)
Espinoza
Result 1-1 T. Rodriguez

82: 29th April 1970
v MEXICO *Leon*
Fernandez
Perez (sub Aguirre)
Paez
De los Santos
F. Lasso
Valencia
Gauna
J. Bolanos (sub V. Lecaro)
De Maria
Aguirre
Rolon
Result 2-4 Aguirre, Rolon

83: 3rd May 1970
v MEXICO *Toluca*
Fernandez
Aguirre (sub Gallardo)
Paez
Valencia
F. Lasso
De Maria (sub Montenegro)
Gauna
De los Santos
Aguirre (sub V. Lecaro)
Rolon
J. Bolanos
Result 2-3 Rolon 2

84: 24th May 1970
v ENGLAND *Quito*
E. Mejia
Utreras
Campoverde
E. Portilla
Valencia
J. Bolanos
Cardenas
W. Munoz (sub M.V. Cabezas)
Penaherrera
P. Carrera (sub Rodriguez)
T. Larrea
Result 0-2

85: 11th June 1972
v PORTUGAL *Natal*
C. Delgado
Cardenas
Noriega (sub Guerrero)
J. Camacho
V. Pelaez
J. Bolanos
H. Morales (sub Coronel)
C. Mantilla
F. Lasso
A. Spencer
I. Estupinan
Result 0-3

86: 14th June 1972
v CHILE *Natal*
C. Delgado
Cardenas
Noriega
J. Camacho
V. Pelaez
J. Bolanos (sub H. Morales)
Coronel
C. Mantilla
F. Lasso
A. Spencer (sub I. Estupinan)
M. Guime
Result 1-2 F. Lasso

87: 19th June 1972
v REPUBLIC OF IRELAND *Natal*
Maldonado
Cardenas
J. Camacho
Guerrero
V. Pelaez
Noriega
Coronel
J. Bolanos
F. Lasso
I. Estupinan
M. Guime
Result 2-3 Coronel, I. Estupinan

88: 21st June 1972
v IRAN *Recife*
Maldonado
V. Pelaez
Guerrero
J. Camacho
J. Ortiz
J. Bolanos
Coronel
C. Mantilla
F. Lasso
A. Spencer
M. Guime
Result 1-1 F. Lasso

89: 18th February 1973
v EAST GERMANY *Quito*
E. Mejia (sub E. Aguirre)
V. Pelaez
E. Portilla
J. Camacho
J. Ortiz
J. Tapia
H. Morales
I. Estupinan
F. Lasso
P. Carrera
M. Guime (sub D. Mina)
Result 1-1 J. Tapia

90: 24th April 1973
v CHILE *Guayaquil*
E. Mejia
V. Pelaez
E. Portilla
E. Enriquez
R. Tobar (sub J. Ortiz)
J. Tapia
W. Parraga
C. Mantilla (sub J. Tenorio)
I. Estupinan
G. Castaneda
M. Guime
Result 1-1 M. Guime

91: 29th April 1973
v BOLIVIA *La Paz*
E. Mejia (sub E. Mendez)
R. Tobar
J. Camacho
E. Portilla
V. Pelaez
W. Parraga
J. Tapia
J. Tenorio
F. Lasso
I. Estupinan
M. Guime
Result 3-3 I. Estupinan 2, M. Guime

92: 6th May 1973
v BOLIVIA *Quito*
E. Mendez
V. Pelaez
J. Camacho
E. Portilla
R. Tobar (sub J. Ortiz)
W. Parraga
J. Tapia (sub J. Bayona)
J. Tenorio (sub C. Mantilla)
F. Lasso
I. Estupinan
M. Guime
Result 0-0

93: 12th May 1973
v HAITI *Port au Prince*
E. Mendez
E. Portilla
J. Camacho
M. Perez
J. Ortiz (sub R. Tobar)
W. Parraga
J. Tapia
F. Lasso
C. Mantilla (sub V. Martinez)
I. Estupinan
M. Guime (sub G. Castaneda)
Result 2-1 I. Estupinan, C. Mantilla

94: 15th May 1973
v HAITI *Port au Prince*
E. Mendez
V. Pelaez
J. Camacho
J. Ortiz
E. Portilla
Noriega (sub R. Guerrero)
P. Carrera
J. Bolanos (sub M. Guime)
F. Lasso
I. Estupinan
W. Munoz
Result 0-1

95: 21st June 1973
v COLOMBIA *Bogota*
E. Mendez
V. Pelaez
E. Portilla
Noriega
J. Ortiz
M.V. Cabezas (sub W. Munoz)
J. Bolanos
J. Camacho (sub P. Carrera)
F. Lasso
I. Estupinan
M. Guime
Result 1-1 J. Ortiz

96: 28th June 1973
v COLOMBIA *Guayaquil*
E. Mendez
V. Pelaez
E. Portilla
Noriega
J. Ortiz
J. Bolanos
J. Camacho (sub G. Castaneda)
W. Munoz (sub P. Carrera)
F. Lasso
I. Estupinan
M. Guime
Result 1-1 W. Munoz (pen)

97: 1st July 1973
v URUGUAY *Quito*
E. Mendez
V. Pelaez
E. Portilla
Noriega
R. Tobar
J. Camacho
J. Bolanos
P. Carrera (sub Bayona)
F. Lasso
I. Estupinan
M. Guime (sub W. Munoz)
Result 1-2 I. Estupinan

98: 8th July 1973
v URUGUAY *Montevideo*
E. Mendez
M. Perez (sub R. Tobar)
E. Portilla (sub F. Lasso)
Noriega
V. Pelaez
J. Camacho
J. Bolanos
R. Guerrero
I. Estupinan
J. Tenorio
M. Guime
Result 0-4

99: 22nd June 1975
v PERU *Quito*
C. Delgado
V. Pelaez (sub W. Guevara)
J. Camacho
F. Carrera
F. Klinger
C. Ron (sub M.V. Cabezas)
J. Tapia
P. Carrera
G. Castaneda (sub W. Gomez)
F. Lasso
F. Paz y Mino
Result 6-0 F. Paz y Mino 2, G. Castaneda,
F. Lasso 2, P. Carrera

100: 25th June 1975
v PERU *Guayaquil*
C. Delgado
V. Pelaez
J. Camacho
R. Guerrero
F. Klinger
C. Ron
J. Tapia
G. Castaneda
F. Lasso
P. Carrera
F. Paz y Mino (sub W. Gomez)
Result 1-0 C. Ron

101: 1st July 1975
v PERU *Lima*
C. Delgado
V. Pelaez
J. Camacho
F. Carrera (Sent Off 43)
F. Klinger
M.V. Cabezas
J. Tapia
C. Ron
G. Castaneda
F. Lasso
F. Paz y Mino (sub R. Guerrero)
Result 0-2

102: 9th July 1975
v BOLIVIA *Cochabamba*
C. Delgado
V. Pelaez
J. Camacho
F. Carrera
F. Klinger
J. Tapia (Sent Off 89)
P. Carrera
C. Ron
G. Castaneda
F. Lasso (sub W. Gomez)
F. Paz y Mino (sub G. Tapia)
Result 0-1

103: 24th July 1975
v PARAGUAY *Guayaquil*
C. Delgado
V. Pelaez
J. Camacho
M. Perez
F. Klinger
C. Ron
J. Tapia (sub M. Cabezas)
P. Carrera (sub R. Tobar)
G. Castaneda
F. Lasso
G. Tapia
Result 2-2 F. Lasso, G. Castaneda

104: 27th July 1975
v COLOMBIA *Quito*
C. Delgado
V. Pelaez
J. Camacho
M. Perez
F. Klinger
C. Ron
J. Tapia (sub M. Cabezas (sub R. Tobar))
G. Castaneda
F. Lasso
P. Carrera
G. Tapia
Result 1-3 P. Carrera

105: 7th August 1975
v COLOMBIA *Bogota*
C. Delgado
F. Klinger
F. Carrera
J. Camacho
V. Pelaez
R. Tobar (sub F. Paz y Mino)
M. Cabezas (Sent Off 8)
J. Tapia
F. Lasso
P. Carrera
G. Castaneda
Result 0-2

106: 10th August 1975
v PARAGUAY *Asuncion*
M. Vera
V. Pelaez
J. Camacho
F. Carrera
F. Klinger
J. Tapia (sub W. Guevara)
R. Tobar
P. Carrera
G. Gastaneda
F. Lasso
F. Paz y Mino
Result 1-3 G. Castaneda

107: 20th October 1976
v URUGUAY *Quito*
Garcia
W. Mendez
E. Figueroa
F. Carrera
F. Klinger
J.C. Gomez (sub Torres)
V. Ron (sub J. Tenorio)
J. Villafuerte
W. Nieves
A. Liciardi
F. Paz y Mino
Result 2-2 A. Liciardi, J. Villafuerte

108: 4th January 1977
v URUGUAY *Montevideo*
C. Delgado (Sent Off 50)
J. Ortiz
J. Camacho
F. Carrera
W. Mendez
L. Granda (Sent Off 78)
J. Villafuerte (Sent Off 78)
J. Carlos (Sent Off 78)
V. Ron
A. Liciardi (sub E. Garcia, Sent Off 78)
W. Nieves
Result 1-1 A. Liciardi   Game was abandoned as Ecuador had only 6 players left on the field.

109: 9th January 1977
v PARAGUAY *Asuncion*
C. Delgado
W. Mendez
F. Carrera
J. Camacho
J. Ortiz
L. Granda
J. Tenorio (sub C.T. Garces)
J. Villafuerte
V. Ron (sub C. Mantilla)
A. Liciardi
W. Nieves
Result 0-2

110: 16th January 1977
v COLOMBIA *Bogota*
C. Delgado
W. Mendez
J. Camacho
F. Villena
F. Klinger
J.C. Gomez
L. Granda (sub J. Tenorio)
J. Villafuerte
A. Liciardi (sub F. Paz y Mino)
V. Ron
W. Nieves
Result 1-0 A. Liciardi

111: 20th January 1977
v VENEZUELA *Acarigua*
C. Delgado
W. Mendez
E. Figueroa
F. Villena (Sent Off 80)
F. Klinger
J.C. Gomez
L. Granda (sub F. Paz y Mino)
J. Villafuerte
V. Ron
A. Liciardi
W. Nieves (sub C. Mantilla)
Result 0-1

112: 26th January 1977
v COLOMBIA *Quito*
C. Delgado
W. Mendez
E. Figueroa
F. Villena
F. Klinger
J.C. Gomez
J. Villafuerte (sub L. Granda)
W. Nieves
A. Liciardi
V. Ron
F. Paz y Mino (sub C. Mantilla)
Result 4-1 J. Villafuerte, A. Liciardi 2, V. Ron

113: 13th February 1977
v PARAGUAY *Quito*
C. Delgado
W. Mendez
F. Carrera
F. Villena
F. Klinger (sub J. Ortiz)
J. Tenorio (sub F. Paz y Mino)
J. Villafuerte
L. Granda
V. Ron
A. Liciardi
W. Nieves (sub C. Mantilla)
Result 2-1 A. Liciardi 2

114: 20th February 1977
v PERU *Quito*
C. Delgado
W. Mendez
F. Villena
F. Carrera
F. Klinger
J. Villafuerte
L. Granda (sub C. Mantilla)
J.C. Gomez (sub F. Paz y Mino)
V. Ron
A. Liciardi
W. Nieves
Result 1-1 F. Paz y Mino

115: 27th February 1977
v CHILE *Guayaquil*
C. Delgado
W. Mendez
F. Carrera
Campoverde
F. Klinger
J.C. Gomez
J. Tenorio (sub L. Granda)
J. Villafuerte
V. Ron
A. Liciardi (sub F. Paz y Mino)
W. Nieves
Result 0-1

116: 12th March 1977
v PERU *Lima*
Garcia
W. Mendez
F. Carrera
F. Villena
F. Klinger
L. Granda
J. Villafuerte
E. Figueroa (sub C. Mantilla)
V. Ron
F. Paz y Mino
W. Nieves
Result 0-4

117: 20th March 1977
v CHILE *Santiago*
Pinillos
J. Ortiz
F. Carrera
Caicedo
F. Klinger
J.C. Gomez
L. Granda (sub E. Figueroa)
J. Villafuerte
V. Ron
C. Mantilla
F. Paz y Mino (sub W. Nieves)
Result 0-3

118: 13th June 1979
v CHILE *Santiago*
M. Rodriguez
F. Perlaza
E. Figueroa (sub J. Bardales)
M. Perez
L. Escalante
C. Ron
C.T. Garces (sub J. Paes)
J. Villafuerte
R. Aguirre (sub R. Parraga)
V. Ron
C. Mantilla
Result 0-0

119: 21st June 1979
v CHILE *Guayaquil*
M. Rodriguez
F. Perlaza
J. Bardales
J. Paes
L. Escalante
C. Ron
J. Villafuerte (sub J.L. Alarcon)
C.T. Garces
R. Parraga (sub M. Tenorio)
V. Ron (sub L. Granda)
C. Mantilla
Result 2-1 C.T. Garces, V. Ron

120: 11th July 1979
v PERU *Lima*
M. Rodriguez
F. Perlaza
J. Paes
J. Bardales
F. Klinger
C.T. Garces
C. Ron
J. Villafuerte
R. Aguirre (sub M. Tenorio)
C. Mantilla
V. Ron
Result 1-2 C. Mantilla

121: 8th August 1979
v PERU *Quito*
M. Rodriguez
F. Perlaza
M. Perez (sub F. Burbano)
E. Figueroa
F. Klinger
J. Paes
J. Villafuerte (sub J. Madrunero)
L. Granda (sub J. Bardales)
M. Tenorio
J.L. Alarcon
C. Mantilla
Result 2-1 J.L. Alarcon, F. Perlaza

122: 29th August 1979
v PARAGUAY *Quito*
M. Rodriguez
F. Perlaza (sub J. Granda)
M. Perez
J. Paes
F. Klinger
J. Villafuerte (sub J.L. Alarcon)
C. Ron
C.T. Garces
M. Tenorio
V. Ron
C. Mantilla
Result 1-2 C.T. Garces (pen)

123: 5th September 1979
v URUGUAY *Quito*
M. Rodriguez
F. Perlaza
M. Perez
J. Paes
F. Klinger
C. Ron
C.T. Garces
L. Granda
M. Tenorio (sub J. Villafuerte)
J.L. Alarcon (sub V. Ron)
J. Madrunero
Result 2-1 M. Tenorio, J.L. Alarcon

124: 13th September 1979
v PARAGUAY *Asuncion*
M. Rodriguez
F. Perlaza
J. Paes
M. Perez
F. Klinger
C. Ron
C.T. Garces
L. Granda
J. Madrunero (sub C. Mantilla)
J.L. Alarcon
M. Tenorio (sub V. Ron)
Result 0-2

125: 16th September 1979
v URUGUAY *Montevideo*
M. Rodriguez
F. Perlaza
E. Figueroa
J. Paes
F. Klinger
L. Granda (Sent Off)
C. Ron (Sent Off)
C.T. Garces (sub J.L. Alarcon)
M. Tenorio
V. Ron
C. Mantilla
Result 1-2 F. Klinger

126: 28th January 1981
v BULGARIA *Quito*
E. Gonzalez
J. Quinteros (sub C. Carrion)
D. Altafuya
E. Figueroa (sub L. Corrales)
E. Mesias
L. Granda (sub A. Vicuna)
C.T. Garces (sub J. Cardenas)
J. Villafuerte
F. Baldeon
V. Ron
J. Valencia (sub A. Arias)
Result 1-3 E. Mesias

127: 14th February 1981
v BRAZIL *Quito*
F. Valdivieso
F. Perlaza
L. Corrales
J. Landeta
E. Mesias
C.T. Garces (sub L. Granda)
W. Parraga
J. Villafuerte (sub V. Ron)
M. Tenorio
G. Revelo (sub L. Quinonez)
J. Madrunero
Result 0-6

128: 17th May 1981
v PARAGUAY *Guayaquil*
C. Delgado
F. Perlaza
J. Paes
E. Figueroa (sub O. Klinger)
D. Valencia
B. Parraga
J. Villafuerte
P. Carrera (sub F. Burbano)
M. Tenorio
L. Quinonez
W. Nieves
Result 1-0 O. Klinger

129: 24th May 1981
v CHILE *Guayaquil*
C. Delgado
F. Perlaza
O. Klinger
J. Paes
D. Valencia
B. Parraga
P. Carrera (sub G. Revelo)
J. Villafuerte
M. Tenorio
L. Quinonez
W. Nieves (sub F. Paz y Mino)
Result 0-0

130: 31st May 1981
v PARAGUAY *Asuncion*
C. Delgado
F. Perlaza
J. Paes
O. Klinger
D. Valencia
E. Figueroa
F. Burbano (sub M. Tenorio)
B. Parraga
P. Carrera
L. Quinonez
W. Nieves
Result 1-3 W. Nieves

131: 14th June 1981
v CHILE *Santiago*
C. Delgado
F. Perlaza
J. Paes
E. Figueroa
D. Valencia (Sent Off 86)
J. Villafuerte
B. Parraga
O. Klinger
M. Tenorio
L. Quinonez
W. Nieves
Result 0-2

132: 26th July 1983
v COLOMBIA *Quito*
C. Delgado
O. Narvaez
W. Armas
O. Klinger
H. Maldonado
T. Quinteros
J. Villafuerte
P. Carrera (sub H. Cuvi)
M. Tenorio
L. Quinonez
G. Cantos
Result 0-0

133: 29th July 1983
v COLOMBIA *Bogota*
C. Delgado
O. Narvaez
W. Armas
O. Klinger
H. Maldonado
J. Villafuerte
B. Ruiz
L. Granda (sub G. Vasquez)
M. Tenorio
L. Quinonez
C. Gorozabel
Result 0-0

134: 10th August 1983
v ARGENTINA *Quito*
C. Delgado
O. Narvaez
O. Klinger
W. Armas
H. Maldonado
P. Carrera (sub G. Vasquez)
J.J. Vega
J. Villafuerte
M. Tenorio
L. Quinonez (sub V. Ron (Sent Off 69))
C. Gorozabel
Result 2-2 G. Vasquez, J.J. Vega

135: 17th August 1983
v BRAZIL *Quito*
C. Delgado
O. Narvaez
O. Klinger
W. Armas
H. Maldonado
G. Vasquez
J.J. Vega (sub P. Carrera)
L. Granda
M. Tenorio
J. Villafuerte
C. Gorozabel (sub L. Quinonez)
Result 0-1

136: 1st September 1983
v BRAZIL *Sao Paulo*
C. Delgado
O. Narvaez
O. Klinger
W. Armas
H. Maldonado
T. Quinteros
L. Granda
G. Vasquez (sub H. Cuvi)
J. Villafuerte
M. Tenorio
L. Quinonez
Result 0-5

137: 7th September 1983
v ARGENTINA *Buenos Aires*
I. Rodriguez
Encalada
W. Armas
O. Klinger
H. Maldonado
J.J. Vega
T. Quinteros
B. Ruiz
Ron
L. Quinonez
H. Cuvi
Result 2-2 L. Quinonez, H. Maldonado (pen)

138: 15th January 1984
v CHILE *Guayaquil*
I. Rodriguez
J. Moran
W. Armas
W. Valdez
O. Narvaez (sub F. Brazo)
H. Castillo (sub L. Floril)
J.F. Minda (sub R. Valencia)
H. Cuvi
G. Mera (sub G. Cajas)
J. Cardenas
L. Ordonez
Result 1-1 J. Cardenas (pen)

139: 18th January 1984
v POLAND *Guayaquil*
I. Rodriguez
M. King
W. Armas
H. Quinonez
F. Bravo
A. Arias (sub J. Cardenas)
H. Cuvi
J.J. Vega (sub H. Valencia)
G. Cajas (sub M. Arguello)
R. Valencia
L. Ordonez
Result 1-1 R. Valencia

140: 22nd January 1984
v ROMANIA *Guayaquil*
W. Guerrero
M. King
H. Valencia (sub W. Armas)
H. Quinonez
F. Bravo
A. Arias
J.J. Vega (sub H. Castillo)
H. Cuvi (sub L. Floril)
M. Arguello (sub G. Mera)
J. Cardenas (sub R. Valencia)
L. Ordonez
Result 1-3 R. Valencia

141: 30th November 1984
v U.S.A. *New York*
I. Rodriguez
F. Perlaza
O. Klinger
L. Preciado
H. Maldonado
E. De Negri
C.T. Garces
J. Villafuerte (sub H. Cuvi)
F. Baldeon (sub V. Ron)
L. Quinonez (sub J. Moreno)
H. Benitez
Result 0-0

142: 2nd December 1984
v U.S.A. *Miami*
I. Rodriguez
F. Perlaza
O. Klinger
L. Preciado
H. Maldonado
J. Villafuerte (sub C.T. Garces)
H. Cuvi
E. De Negri
F. Baldeon
L. Quinonez
H. Benitez (sub V. Ron)
Result 2-2 H. Cuvi, H.Benitez

143: 4th December 1984
v MEXICO *Los Angeles*
I. Rodriguez
F. Perlaza
O. Klinger
L. Preciado
H. Maldonado
E. De Negri
M. Hurtado
H. Cuvi
J. Villafuerte
F. Baldeon (sub H. Benitez)
L. Quinonez
Result 2-3 E. De Negri, J. Villafuerte

144: 7th December 1984
v HONDURAS *Tegucigalpa*
P. Latino
F. Perlaza
O. Klinger
H. Quinonez
H. Maldonado
E. De Negri
H. Cuvi
C.T. Garces
J. Villafuerte
F. Baldeon (sub L. Quinonez)
V. Ron (sub H. Benitez)
Result 0-0

145: 9th December 1984
v GUATEMALA *Guatemala*
I. Rodriguez
F. Perlaza
O. Klinger
H. Quinonez (Sent Off)
H. Maldonado
M. Hurtado
H. Cuvi
J. Villafuerte
C.T. Garces (sub J. Moreno)
F. Baldeon
L. Quinonez
Result 0-1

146: 12th December 1984
v EL SALVADOR *San Salvador*
I. Rodriguez
F. Perlaza
O. Klinger
L. Preciado
H. Maldonado
E. De Negri
M. Hurtado
J. Villafuerte
H. Cuvi
L. Quinonez
F. Baldeon
Result 1-1 L. Quinonez

147: 6th February 1985
v EAST GERMANY *Guayaquil*
I. Rodriguez
L. Capurro
O. Klinger
L. Preciado (sub W. Armas)
H. Maldonado (sub J.J. Vega)
E. De Negri
J. Villafuerte (sub C.T. Garces)
M. Hurtado (sub G. Vasquez)
F. Baldeon
H. Benitez
H. Cuvi
Result 2-3 F. Baldeon, H. Benitez

148: 10th February 1985
v EAST GERMANY *Quito*
P. Latino
L. Capurro
O. Klinger (Sent Off)
W. Armas
H. Maldonado
H. Cuvi
J. Villafuerte
E. De Negri
F. Baldeon
H. Benitez (sub J.J. Vega)
F. Paz y Mino
Result 3-2 H. Benitez 2, H. Maldonado

149: 17th February 1985
v FINLAND *Ambato*
P. Latino
L. Capurro
H. Quinonez
W. Armas
H. Maldonado
H. Cuvi
J. Villafuerte
E. De Negri
F. Baldeon
H. Benitez (sub G. Vasquez)
F. Paz y Mino (sub J.V. Moreno)
Result 3-1 F. Paz y Mino, H. Benitez 2

150: 21st February 1985
v BOLIVIA *Quito*
P. Latino
F. Perlaza
H. Quinonez
W. Armas
H. Maldonado
M. Hurtado
E. De Negri (sub J.J. Vega)
J. Villafuerte
G. Vasquez
H. Benitez
F. Paz y Mino
Result 3-0 H. Maldonado, H. Benitez, J. Villafuerte

151: 3rd March 1985
v CHILE *Quito*
I. Rodriguez
F. Perlaza
H. Quinonez (Sent Off)
W. Armas
H. Maldonado
M. Hurtado
E. De Nergri
J. Villafuerte (sub H. Cuvi)
F. Baldeon
H. Benitez
J.V. Moreno (sub L. Quinonez)
Result 1-1 H. Maldonado (pen)

152: 10th March 1985
v URUGUAY *Montevideo*
I. Rodriguez
F. Perlaza
W. Armas
O. Klinger
H. Maldonado
J. Villafuerte
M. Hurtado
E. De Negri
H. Cuvi
F. Baldeon (sub H. Benitez)
L. Quinonez (sub G. Vasquez)
Result 1-2 H. Cuvi

153: 17th March 1985
v CHILE *Santiago*
I. Rodriguez
H. Maldonado (sub J. Valencia)
W. Armas
O. Klinger
F. Perlaza
J. Villafuerte
M. Hurtado
E. De Negri
H. Cuvi
H. Benitez
F. Baldeon
Result 2-6 F. Baldeon 2

154: 21st March 1985
v PERU *Lima*
P. Latino
F. Perlaza
O. Klinger
L. Perciado
L. Capurro
J.J. Vega (sub E. De Negri)
M. Hurtado
H. Cuvi (sub J. Villafuerte)
G. Vasquez (sub F. Baledon)
L. Quinonez (sub H. Benitez)
J. Valencia
Result 0-1

155: 31st March 1985
v URUGUAY *Quito*
I. Rodriguez (sub P. Latino)
L. Capurro
O. Klinger
W. Armas
H. Maldonado
M. Hurtado (sub J. Valencia)
E. De Negri
J. Villafuerte
F. Baldeon
L. Quinonez (sub T. Amarilla)
H. Cuvi
Result 0-2

156: 8th March 1987
v CUBA *Havana*
H.L. Chiriboga
F. Bravo
H. Quinonez
W. Macias
L. Mosquera
J. Sanchez (sub C. Alcivar)
E. Dominguez
K. Farjardo
P. Marsetti (sub F. Barreto)
A. Aguinaga
R. Aviles
Result 0-0

157: 31st March 1987
v CUBA *Machala*
H.L. Chiriboga
L. Carrion
K. Fajardo
H. Quinonez
C. Alcivar
E. Dominguez
W. Macias
P. Marsetti
E. Vaca
R. Aviles
S. Batioja (sub D. Cordova)
Result 0-1

158: 2nd April 1987
v CUBA *Azogues*
C. Enriquez (sub H.L. Chiriboga)
P. Marin
W. Macias
K. Fajardo
L. Carrion
E. Dominguez
E. Verduga
A. Aguinaga
R. Aviles (sub D. Cordova)
S. Batioja (sub P. Marsetti)
P. Munoz
Result 0-0

159: 15th April 1987
v PERU *Lima*
H.L. Chiriboga
L. Carrion
A. Macias
K. Fajardo
J.C. Jacome
E. Dominguez (Sent Off 30)
P. Marsetti (sub P. Marin)
L. Mosquera (sub E. Verduga)
R. Aviles
P. Munoz (sub R. Marquez)
J. Guerrero
Result 1-0 R. Aviles

160: 11th June 1987
v COLOMBIA *Medellin*
C.L. Morales
J.C. Jacome
U. Canga
K. Farjardo
L. Capurro
E. Dominguez
P. Marin (sub P. Marsetti)
H. Cuvi (sub A. Aguinaga)
F. Baldeon (sub G. Mera (Sent Off))
L. Quinonez
R. Aviles
Result 0-1

161: 14th June 1987
v COLOMBIA *Guayaquil*
C.L. Morales
L. Mosquera
K. Fajardo
W. Macias
L. Capurro
H. Cuvi
P. Marin (sub F. Baldeon)
A. Aguinaga (sub P. Marsetti)
E. Dominguez
L. Quinonez
R. Aviles
*Result 3-0 L. Quinonez, F. Baldeon,
P. Marsetti*

162: 19th June 1987
v URUGUAY *Montevideo*
C.L. Morales
L. Capurro
W. Macias
K. Fajardo
L. Mosquera
E. Dominguez
A. Aguinaga (sub G. Mera)
H. Cuvi (sub P. Marsetti)
P. Marin
L. Quinonez
F. Baldeon
Result 1-2 P. Marsetti

163: 21st June 1987
v BRAZIL *Florianopolis*
C.L. Morales
L. Mosquera
K. Farjardo
W. Macias
L. Capurro
E. Dominguez (sub R. Aviles)
P. Marin
H. Cuvi (sub P. Marsetti)
G. Vasquez
L. Quinonez
F. Baldeon (sub G. Mera)
Result 1-4 G. Mera

164: 7th September 1988
v PARAGUAY *Guayaquil*
A. Cevallos (sub H.L. Chiriboga)
U. Quinteros
W. Macias
J.C. Suarez
S. Pazmino (sub L. Capurro)
P. Marin (sub E. Dominguez)
F. Delgado (sub H. Cuvi)
P. Marsetti
P.M. Munoz
B. Tenorio
N. Guerrero (sub L. Mosquera)
Result 1-5 H. Cuvi (pen)

165: 13th September 1988
v CHILE *La Serena*
C.L. Morales
K. Fajardo
W. Macias
H. Quinonez
L. Capurro
E. Dominguez
H. Cuvi
P. Marsetti
P.M. Munoz (sub J.F. Minda)
B. Tenorio
R. Aviles
Result 1-3 H. Cuvi

166: 27th September 1988
v URUGUAY *Asuncion*
C.L. Morales
J. Izquierdo
H. Quinonez
T. Quinteros (sub W. Macias)
L. Capurro (Sent Off)
K. Fajardo
A. Aguinaga (sub J.F. Minda)
H. Cuvi
P. Masetti
B. Tenorio
R. Aviles
Result 1-2 J. Izquierdo

167: 29th September 1988
v CHILE *Asuncion*
C.L. Morales
J. Izquierdo
H. Quinonez
W. Macias
T. Quinteros
K. Fajardo
P. Masetti
A. Aguinaga
H. Cuvi
B. Tenorio
R. Aviles
Result 0-0
(2-3 penalties – H. Cuvi, P. Masetti)

168: 29th January 1989
v CHILE *Guayaquil*
C.L. Morales
T. Quinteros (sub C. Alcivar)
W. Macias
H. Quinonez
L. Capurro
K. Fajardo
P. Marsetti (sub J.F. Minda)
A. Aguinaga
R. Aviles
B. Tenorio (sub W.E. Verduga)
H. Cuvi (sub J. Cardenas)
Result 1-0 R. Aviles

169: 15th March 1989
v BRAZIL *Cuiba*
C.L. Morales
C. Alcivar (sub T. Quinonez)
H. Quinonez
W. Macias
L. Capurro
W.E. Verduga (sub C. Munoz)
K. Fajardo (sub J. Montanero)
P. Marsetti (sub N. Guerrero)
H. Cuvi (sub J.C. Rosero)
R. Aviles
B. Tenorio (Sent Off)
Result 0-1

170: 13th April 1989
v ARGENTINA *Guayaquil*
C.L. Morales
C. Alcivar
H. Quinonez
W. Macias
L. Capurro
K. Fajardo
W.E. Verduga (sub J.C. Rosero)
P. Masetti (sub T. Quinteros)
H. Cuvi
R. Aviles
C. Munoz (sub N. Guerrero)
Result 2-2 R. Aviles, H. Cuvi (pen)

171: 3rd May 1989
v URUGUAY *Montevideo*
C.L. Morales
J. Izquierdo (sub C. Alcivar)
H. Quinonez
W. Marcias
L. Capurro
K. Fajardo
H. Cuvi
P. Marsetti (sub J.C. Rosero)
A. Aguinaga
B. Tenorio (sub C. Munoz)
R. Aviles
Result 1-3 R. Aviles

172: 23rd May 1989
v URUGUAY *Quito*
C.L. Morales
J. Izquierdo
H. Quinonez
W. Macias
L. Capurro
K. Fajardo
J.C. Rosero
H. Cuvi (sub N. Guerrero)
A. Aguinaga (sub C. Munoz)
B. Tenorio
R. Aviles
Result 1-1 R. Aviles

173: 20th June 1989
v PERU *Port of Spain*
V. Mendoza
C. Alcivar
W. Marcias
H. Quinonez
L. Capurro (Sent Off)
K. Fajardo (sub R. Aviles)
W.E. Verduga (sub C. Munoz)
P. Marsetti (sub J. Montanero)
N. Guerrero (Sent Off)
H. Bentiez
B. Tenorio (sub H. Cuvi)
Result 1-2 N. Guerrero

174: 2nd July 1989
v URUGUAY *Goiania*
C.L. Morales
J. Izquierdo
W. Macias
H. Quinonez
L. Capurro
K. Fajardo
H. Cuvi
A. Aguinaga (sub P. Marsetti)
J.C. Rosero
R. Aviles
B. Tenorio (sub E. Benitez)
Result 1-0 E. Benitez

175: 4th July 1989
v ARGENTINA *Goiania*

C.L. Morales
J. Izquierdo
W. Macias
H. Quinonez
L. Capurro (Sent Off)
K. Fajardo
J.C. Rosero
H. Cuvi
A. Aguinaga
B. Tenorio (sub E. Benitez)
R. Aviles

Result 0-0

176: 6th July 1989
v BOLIVIA *Goiania*

C.L. Morales
J. Izquierdo
W. Macias
H. Quinonez
C. Alcivar (sub E. Benitez)
K. Fajardo
J.C. Rosero
A. Aguinaga
H. Cuvi
R. Aviles
B. Tenorio (sub P. Marsetti)

Result 0-0

177: 10th July 1989
v CHILE *Goiania*

C.L. Morales
J. Izquierdo
W. Macias
H. Quinonez
L. Capurro
K. Fajardo (sub J. Montanero)
J.C. Rosero
A. Aguinaga
H. Cuvi
R. Aviles
B. Tenorio (sub E. Benitez)

Result 1-2 R. Aviles

178: 20th August 1989
v COLOMBIA *Barranquilla*

C.L. Morales
J. Izquierdo
W. Macias
H. Quinonez
L. Capurro
K. Fajardo
J.C. Rosero
H. Cuvi (sub P. Marsetti)
A. Aguinaga
R. Aviles
E. Benitez (sub B. Tenorio)

Result 0-2

179: 3rd September 1989
v COLOMBIA *Guayaquil*

C.L. Morales
J. Izquierdo
T. Quinteros
H. Quinonez
L. Capurro
K. Fajardo
J.C. Rosero (sub E. Benitez)
H. Cuvi (sub E. Verduga)
A. Aguinaga
R. Aviles
B. Tenorio

Result 0-0

180: 10th September 1989
v PARAGUAY *Asuncion*

C.L. Morales
F. Bravo
T. Quinteros
H. Quinonez
L. Capurro
K. Fajardo
J.C. Rosero (sub H. Cuvi)
A. Aguinaga (sub B. Tenorio)
N. Guerrero
R. Aviles
C. Munoz

Result 1-2 R. Aviles

181: 24th September 1989
v PARAGUAY *Guayaquil*
V. Mendoza
F. Bravo
W. Macias
H. Quinonez
L. Capurro
K. Fajardo
P. Marsetti (sub E. Verduga)
A. Aguinaga
C. Munoz (Sent Off)
R. Aviles
N. Guerrero (sub B. Tenorio)
Result 3-1 A. Aguinaga, P. Marsetti, R. Aviles

184: 25th June 1991
v PERU *Quito*
E. Ramirez
J. Rivero
B. Tenorio
L. Capurro
J. Guerrero
F. Bravo
J.C. Garay (sub M. Uquillas)
N. Carcelen (sub R. Aviles)
S. Batioia (sub W. Macias)
A. Aguinaga
C. Munoz (sub R. Burbano)
Result 2-2 N. Carcelen, C. Munoz

182: 6th June 1991
PERU *Lima*
E. Ramirez
L. Capurro
J. Montanero
B. Tenorio
J. Guerrero
J.C. Garay
I. Ron (sub A. Fernandez)
F. Bravo
N. Carcelen (sub W. Macias)
C. Munoz
R. Burbano (sub J. Guaman)
Result 1-0 I. Ron

185: 30th June 1991
v CHILE *Santiago*
E. Ramirez
L. Capurro
B. Tenorio
C. Rivera
J. Guerrero (sub M. Uquillas)
F. Bravo
C. Munoz (sub R. Burbano)
N. Carcelen
J.C. Garay (sub A. Fernandez)
R. Aviles
A. Aguinaga
Result 1-3 A. Aguinaga

183: 19th June 1991
v CHILE *Quito*
E. Ramirez
C. Rivera
B. Tenorio
L. Capurro
J. Guerrero
F. Bravo
N. Carcelen (sub R. Aviles)
J.C. Garay
I. Ron (sub A. Aguinaga)
R. Burbano (sub M. Uquillas)
E. Hurtado (sub C. Munoz)
Result 2-1 J.C. Garay, J. Guerrero

186: 7th July 1991
v COLOMBIA *Valparaiso*
E. Ramirez
J. Montanero
B. Tenorio
L. Capurro
H. Quinonez
F. Bravo
J.C. Garay
N. Carcelen
A. Aguinaga
C. Munoz (sub M. Uquillas)
R. Aviles (sub R. Burbano)
Result 0-1

187: 9th July 1991
v URUGUAY *Vina del Mar*
E. Ramirez
J. Montanero
B. Tenorio
L. Capurro
H. Quinonez
N. Carcelen
J.C. Garay
F. Bravo
A. Aguinaga
C. Munoz (sub R. Burbano)
R. Aviles (sub J. Guerrero)
Result 1-1 A. Aguinaga

188: 13th July 1991
v BOLIVIA *Vina del Mar*
E. Ramirez
J. Montanero
B. Tenorio
L. Capurro
H. Quinonez
F. Bravo
I. Ron
C. Munoz
N. Carcelen (sub R. Burbano)
A. Aguinaga (sub J.C. Garay)
R. Aviles
Result 4-0 A. Aguinaga, R. Aviles 2,
E. Ramirez (pen)

189: 15th July 1991
v BRAZIL *Vina del Mar*
E. Ramirez
J. Montanero
B. Tenorio
L. Capurro
H. Quinonez
F. Bravo
I. Ron
N. Carcelen
A. Aguinaga
C. Munoz
R. Aviles
Result 1-3 C. Munoz

190: 24th May 1992
v GUATEMALA *Guatemala*
J. Espinoza
J. Guerrero
L. Capurro
I. Hurtado
D. Coronel
H. Carabali
N. Carcelen
K. Chala
J.C. Garay
A. Fernandez (sub O. De la Cruz)
E. Hurtado (sub D. Herrera)
Result 1-1 I. Hurtado (pen)

191: 27th May 1992
v COSTA RICA *San Jose*
J. Espinoza
J. Guerrero
L. Capurro
I. Hurtado
D. Coronal
H. Carabali
A. Montano (sub R. Mantilla)
N. Carcelen
A. Fernandez
E. Hurtado
K. Chala
Result 1-2 H. Carabali

192: 4th July 1992
v URUGUAY *Montevideo*
J. Espinoza
R. Noriega (sub H. Carabali)
J. Montanero
I. Hurtado (sub D. Coronel)
L. Capurro
H. Quinonez (sub J.C. Garay)
M. Tenorio
N. Carcelen (sub K. Chala)
A. Fernandez
R. Aviles
C. Munoz
Result 1-3 A. Fernandez

193: 6th August 1992
v COSTA RICA *Guayaquil*
J. Espinoza
R. Noriega
B. Tenorio
L. Capurro
D. Coronel (sub I. Hurtado)
H. Carabali
N. Carcelen
I. Ron (sub O. De la Cruz)
J. Gavica (sub R. Aviles)
A. Fernandez
C. Munoz (sub M. Tenorio)
Result 1-1 B. Tenorio

194: 24th November 1992
v PERU *Lima*
J. Espinoza
H. Ferri
I. Hurtado
L. Capurro
A. Hurtado
H. Carabali
H. Zambrano (sub D. Coronel)
N. Carcelen
A. Fernandez
R. Aviles (sub C. Quinonez)
D. Reascos
Result 1-1 H. Zambrano

195: 27th January 1993
v BELARUS *Guayaquil*
J. Espinoza
C. Munoz
R. Noriega
B. Tenorio
J. Guerrero
H. Carabali (sub I. Hurtado)
N. Carcelen (sub J. Gavica)
A. Fernandez
K. Chala (sub H. Zambrano)
R. Aviles
E. Hurtado (sub M. Tenorio)
Result 1-1 A. Fernandez

196: 31st January 1993
v ROMANIA *Guayaquil*
V. Mendoza (sub F. Cevallos)
C. Munoz
R. Noriega
B. Tenorio
I. Hurtado
H. Carabali
N. Carcelen
A. Fernandez
J. Gavica (sub A. Hurtado)
R. Aviles (sub D. Herrera)
E. Hurtado
Result 3-0 E. Hurtado, J. Gavica, R. Aviles

197: 30th May 1993
v PERU *Quito*
J. Espinoza
C. Munoz
R. Noriega
L. Capurro
J. Montanero (sub H. Quinonez)
H. Carabali
N. Carcelen
J. Gavica (sub D. Coronel)
A. Fernandez (sub J.C. Garay)
K. Chala (sub A. Aguinaga)
L. Cherrez (sub E. Hurtado)
Result 1-0 A. Fernandez

198: 9th June 1993
v CHILE *Quito*
J. Espinoza
C. Munoz
B. Tenorio
L. Capurro (sub R. Noriega)
J. Guerrero
N. Carcelen
H. Carabali
H. Quinonez (sub J. Gavica)
K. Chala
R. Aviles (sub A. Fernandez)
E. Hurtado
Result 1-2 R. Aviles

199: 15th June 1993
v VENEZUELA *Quito*

J. Espinoza
C. Munoz
R. Noriega
L. Capurro
J. Montanero (sub I. Hurtado)
H. Carabali
N. Carcelen
A. Aguinaga
A. Fernandez
R. Aviles (sub J. Gavica)
E. Hurtado

Result 6-1 C. Munoz, R. Noriega, A. Fernandez 2, E. Hurtado, A. Aguinaga

200: 19th June 1993
v U.S.A. *Quito*

J. Espinoza
C. Munoz
R. Noriega (sub B. Tenorio)
L. Capurro
J. Montanero
H. Carabali
N. Carcelen
A. Aguinaga
A. Fernandez
R. Aviles (sub J. Gavica)
E. Hurtado

Result 2-0 R. Aviles, E. Hurtado

201: 22nd June 1993
v URUGUAY *Quito*

J. Espinoza
C. Munoz
R. Noriega
L. Capurro
J. Montanero
H. Carabali
N. Carcelen
A. Aguinaga
A. Fernandez (sub M. Tenorio)
R. Aviles (sub B. Tenorio)
E. Hurtado

Result 2-1 R. Aviles, A. Aguinaga

202: 26th June 1993
v PARAGUAY *Quito*

J. Espinoza
C. Munoz
R. Noriega
L. Capurro
J. Montanero
H. Carabali
N. Carcelen
A. Aguinaga (sub J. Gavica)
A. Fernandez (sub I. Hurtado)
R. Aviles
E. Hurtado

Result 3-0 E. Hurtado, R. Aviles, Ramirez (own goal)

203: 30th June 1993
v MEXICO *Guayaquil*

J. Espinoza
C. Munoz
R. Noriega
L. Capurro
I. Hurtado
H. Carabali
N. Carcelen
A. Aguinaga
A. Fernandez (sub J. Gavica)
R. Aviles
E. Hurtado (sub K. Chala)

Result 0-2

204: 3rd July 1993
v COLOMBIA *Portoviejo*

J. Espinoza
C. Munoz
R. Noriega
L. Capurro
J. Montanero
H. Carabali
N. Carcelen
A. Aguinaga
A. Fernandez (sub B. Tenorio)
R. Aviles
E. Hurtado (sub K. Chala)

Result 0-1

205: 18th July 1993
v BRAZIL *Guayaquil*
J. Espinoza
D. Coronel
R. Noriega
B. Tenorio
L. Capurro
M. Tenorio
N. Carcelen
H. Carabali (sub I. Hurtado)
K. Chala (sub E. Hurtado)
A. Aguinaga
C. Munoz
Result 0-0

206: 1st August 1993
v URUGUAY *Montevideo*
J. Espinoza
D. Coronel
B. Tenorio (sub H. Carabali)
R. Noriega
L. Capurro
M. Tenorio
I. Hurtado
N. Carcelen
A. Aguinaga (sub K. Chala)
C. Munoz
E. Hurtado
Result 0-0

207: 8th August 1993
v VENEZUELA *Quito*
J. Espinoza
D. Coronel (sub E. Zambrano)
J. Montanero
H. Carabali
L. Capurro
I. Hurtado
C. Munoz
N. Carcelen
K. Chala (sub R. Aviles)
A. Fernandez
E. Hurtado
Result 5-0 C. Munoz, E. Hurtado 3, K. Chala

208: 15th August 1993
v BOLIVIA *La Paz*
J. Espinoza
D. Coronel
M. Tenorio
R. Noriega
L. Capurro
H. Carabali
I. Hurtado
N. Carcelen
A. Aguinaga (sub A. Fernandez)
C. Munoz (sub K. Chala)
E. Hurtado
Result 0-1

209: 22nd August 1993
v BRAZIL *Sao Paulo*
J. Espinoza
D. Coronel
I. Hurtado
M. Tenorio
L. Capurro
H. Carabali
N. Carcelen
K. Chala
A. Fernandez (sub J. Gavica)
C. Munoz (sub R. Aviles)
E. Hurtado
Result 0-2

210: 5th September 1993
v URUGUAY *Guayaquil*
J. Espinoza
I. Hurtado (sub R. Aviles)
B. Tenorio
R. Noriega
L. Capurro
H. Carabali
N. Carcelen (sub K. Chala)
A. Aguinaga
J. Gavica
C. Munoz
E. Hurtado
Result 0-1

211: 12th September 1993
v VENEZUELA *Ciudad Guyana*
J. Espinoza
C. Munoz (sub R. Aviles)
R. Noriega
L. Capurro
I. Hurtado
N. Carcelen
D. Coronel
K. Chala (sub J. Gavica)
A. Fernandez
B. Tenorio
E. Hurtado
Result 1-2 B. Tenorio

212: 19th September 1993
v BOLIVIA *Guayaquil*
J. Espinoza
D. Coronel
R. Noriega
I. Hurtado
L. Capurro
M. Tenorio
A. Aguinaga
K. Chala (sub N. Carcelen)
A. Fernandez
C. Munoz (sub J. Gavica)
R. Aviles
Result 1-1 R. Noriega

213: 4th May 1994
v SOUTH KOREA *Boston, U.S.A.*
J. Espinoza
D. Coronel
B. Tenorio
A. Montano
M. Tenorio
L. Capurro
J.C. Garay
K. Fajardo (sub J. Gavica)
K. Chala
I. Ron
C. Vernaza (sub W. Carabali)
Result 2-1 I. Ron 2

214: 25th May 1994
v ARGENTINA *Guayaquil*
J. Espinoza
D. Coronel
A. Montano
B. Tenorio
L. Capurro
H. Carabali (sub N. Carcelen)
K. Fajardo (sub J. Gavica)
M. Tenorio
J.C. Garay
K. Chala (sub C. Vernaza)
I. Ron
Result 1-0 B. Tenorio

215: 30th May 1994
v PERU *Lima*
J. Espinoza
D. Coronel (sub W. Carabali)
B. Tenorio
A. Montano
L. Capurro
Achilie
K. Fajardo
H. Carabali
I. Ron (sub Cubero)
E. Hurtado (sub Maldonado)
A. Delgado
Result 0-2

216: 21st September 1994
v PERU *Machala*
D. Coronel
R. Noriega
L. Capurro
B. Tenorio
M. Tenorio
I. Hurtado
W. Carabali
H. Carabali
A. Fernandez
M. Uquillas
E. Hurtado
Result 0-0

217: 24th May 1995
v SCOTLAND *Tokyo*
F. Cevallos
L. Capurro
R. Noriega
I. Hurtado
J. Guaman
W. Verduga
N. Carcelen
J.C. Garay (sub A. Delgado)
H. Zambrano
E. Hurtado
D. Herrera (sub J. Mora)
Result 1-2 I. Hurtado

218: 28th May 1995
v JAPAN *Tokyo*
F. Cevallos
L. Capurro
M. Tenorio
R. Noriega (sub N. Carcelen)
J. Guaman (sub Ulises de la Cruz)
I. Hurtado
W. Verduga
J.C. Garay
J. Mora (sub H. Zambrano)
E. Hurtado
A. Delgado
Result 0-3

219: 30th June 1995
v PARAGUAY *Asuncion*
F. Cevallos
L. Capurro
R. Noriega
I. Hurtado
J. Guaman
J.C. Garay
H. Quinonez
N. Ascencio (sub A. Aguinaga)
J.C. Garay
E. Diaz
E. Hurtado
Result 0-1

220: 7th July 1995
v BRAZIL *Rivera*
C.L. Morales
J. Guaman (Sent Off)
M. Tenorio
I. Hurtado
L. Capurro
W. Carabali
H. Quinonez
J. Mora (sub N. Ascencio)
A. Aguinaga
E. Diaz (sub P. Hurtado)
E. Hurtado
Result 0-1

221: 10th July 1995
v COLOMBIA *Rivera*
C.L. Morales
D. Coronel
I. Hurtado
M. Tenorio
L. Capurro
W. Carabali (sub J. Mora)
H. Quinonez
D. Herrera (sub J.C. Garay)
A. Aguinaga
P. Hurtado (sub N. Ascencio)
E. Hurtado
Result 0-1

222: 13th July 1995
v PERU *Rivera*
C.L. Morales
J. Guaman
M. Tenorio
I. Hurtado
L. Capurro
J.C. Garay (sub R. Noriega)
H. Quinonez (sub J. Mora)
N. Carcelen (Sent Off)
A. Aguinaga
E. Hurtado
E. Diaz (sub I. Ron)
Result 2-1 E. Diaz, J. Mora

223: 2nd February 1996
v VENEZUELA *Caracas*

J. Cevallos
W. Rivera
M. Tenorio
A. Montano
W. Carabali
A. Obregon
R. Macias (sub R. Burbano)
K. Chala (sub L. Gonzalez)
O. De la Cruz (sub J.C. Garay)
J. Batallas (sub A. Fernandez)
E. Hurtado

Result 1-0 A. Fernandez

224: 11th February 1996
v LEBANON *Beirut*

J. Cevallos
W. Rivera
M. Tenorio
A. Montano
W. Carabali (sub S. Pazmino)
A. Obregon (sub J.C. Garay)
R. Macias (sub L. Gonzalez)
K. Chala (sub P. Hurtado)
J. Batallas
A. Fernandez
E. Hurtado

Result 0-1

225: 16th February 1996
v OMAN *Qatar*

J. Espinoza
W. Rivera
M. Tenorio (sub B. Tenorio)
A. Montano
S. Pazmino
J.C. Garay (sub A. Obregon)
W. Carabali (sub K. Chala)
L. Gonzalez
J. Batallas
A. Fernandez
E. Hurtado (sub P. Hurtado)

Result 2-0 E. Hurtado, A. Fernandez

226: 18th February 1996
v QATAR *Qatar*

J. Espinoza
W. Rivera
M. Tenorio
A. Montano
S. Pazmino
J.C. Garay (sub R. Macias)
W. Carabali (sub K. Chala)
L. Gonzalez
J. Batallas
A. Fernandez (sub R. Burbano)
E. Hurtado

Result 1-1 E. Hurtado

227: 23rd February 1996
v KUWAIT *Qatar*

J. Cevallos
W. Rivera
M. Tenorio (sub B. Tenorio)
A. Montano
S. Pazmino
J.C. Garay
W. Carabali
L. Gonzalez (sub O. De la Cruz)
J. Batallas
A. Fernandez
E. Hurtado (sub P. Hurtado)

Result 3-0 M. Tenorio, E. Hurtado, J. Batallas

228: 25th February 1996
v QATAR *Doha*

J. Cevallos
W. Rivera
M. Tenorio
A. Montano (sub B. Tenorio)
S. Pazmino
J.C. Garay
W. Carabali (sub W. Macias)
L. Gonzalez
J. Batallas (sub R. Burbano)
A. Fernandez
E. Hurtado

Result 2-1 E. Hurtado, A. Fernandez

229: 6th March 1996
v JAPAN *Gifu*
J. Espinoza
W. Rivera
M. Tenorio
A. Montano
S. Pazmino
J.C. Garay (sub A. Obregon)
L. Gonzalez
W. Carabali
G. de Souza
A. Fernandez
E. Hurtado
Result 1-0 E. Hurtado

230: 24th April 1996
v PERU *Guayaquil*
C.L. Morales
W. Rivera
A. Montano
M. Tenorio
L. Capurro
I. Hurtado (sub A. Obregon)
W. Carabali (sub H. Carabali)
G. de Souza
A. Fernandez (sub J. Gavica)
A. Aguinaga
E. Hurtado
Result 4-1 E. Hurtado 2, M. Tenorio,
J. Gavica

231: 2nd June 1996
v ARGENTINA *Quito*
C.L. Morales
W. Rivera
M. Tenorio
A. Montano
L. Capurro
I. Hurtado (sub A. Obregon)
H. Carabali
J. Gavica (sub A. Fernandez)
A. Aguinaga
G. de Souza
E. Hurtado
Result 2-0 A. Montano, E. Hurtado

232: 30th June 1996
v ARMENIA *Tamarindos*
C.L. Morales (sub J. Espinoza)
D. Coronel
A. Montano (sub Matamba)
B. Tenorio
L. Capurro
A. Obregon (sub E. Diaz)
L. Gonzalez
J. Gavica
G. de Souza
A. Fernandez
M. Uquillas (sub W. Sanchez)
Result 3-0 G. de Souza, A. Fernandez,
J. Gavica

233: 7th July 1996
v CHILE *Santiago*
C.L. Morales
W. Rivera
M. Tenorio (sub L. Gonzalez)
A. Montano (sub B. Tenorio)
L. Capurro
H. Carabali
I. Hurtado
A. Obregon (sub A. Fernandez)
Gilson
Aguinaga
E. Hurtado
Result 1-4 A. Aguinaga

234: 16th August 1996
v COSTA RICA *Ambato*
A. Cevallos
J.C. Burbano
H. Quinonez
M. Tenorio
L. Capurro
A. Obregon (sub E. Ordonez)
H. Carabali
J. Gavica
G. Yepez (sub E. Smith)
A. Fernandez
W. Sanchez (sub J. Oleas)
Result 1-1 A. Fernandez

235: 1st September 1996
v VENEZUELA *Quito*
C.L. Morales
W. Rivera
I. Hurtado
M. Tenorio
L. Capurro
H. Carabali
G. de Souza
J. Gavica (sub A. Fernandez)
J. Diaz (sub A. Obregon)
A. Aguinaga
E. Hurtado
Result 1-0 A. Aguinaga

236: 4th October 1996
v JAMAICA *Bellavista*
C.L. Morales (sub A. Cevallos)
J.C. Burbano
A. Montano
M. Tenorio (sub E. Smith)
E. Mendez
I. Hurtado (sub A. Obregon)
H. Carabali (sub J. Diaz)
O. De la Cruz
G. de Souza
A. Fernandez
A. Delgado
Result 2-1 A. Delgado 2

237: 9th October 1996
v COLOMBIA *Quito*
C.L. Morales
W. Rivera
A. Montano
M. Tenorio
L. Capurro
I. Hurtado (sub A. Obregon)
H. Carabali
A. Aguinaga
G. de Souza (sub A. Fernandez)
A. Delgado
E. Hurtado
Result 0-1

238: 23rd October 1996
v MEXICO *Oakland, U.S.A.*
C.L. Morales
J.C. Burbano (sub E. Mendez)
B. Tenorio
A. Montano
H. Quinonez
J. Diaz
H. Carabali
O. De La Cruz
G. de Souza
A. Delgado (sub E. Ordonez)
F. Cuber
Result 1-0 H. Carabali

239: 10th November 1996
v PARAGUAY *Asuncion*
C.L. Morales
W. Rivera
B. Tenorio
A. Montano
H. Quinonez
I. Hurtado
O. De la Cruz
E. Smith
G. de Souza (sub A. Fernandez)
A. Aguinaga
E. Hurtado
Result 0-1

240: 12th January 1997
v BOLIVIA *La Paz*
C.L. Morales
W. Rivera
B. Tenorio
A. Montano
H. Quinonez
I. Hurtado
H. Carabali
O. De la Cruz (sub G. de Souza)
A. Aguinaga
K. Chala (sub A. Delgado)
A. Fernandez (sub E. Hurtado)
Result 0-2

241: 5th February 1997
v MEXICO *La Paz*
Ibarra
W. Rivera
M. Tenorio
L. Capurro
A. Montano
Ruiz
Blandon
G. de Souza
O. de La Cruz
K. Chala (sub A. Fernandez)
A. Delgado
Result 1-3 A. Delgado

242: 12th February 1997
v URUGUAY *Quito*
Ibarra
W. Rivera
A. Montano
I. Hurtado
L. Capurro
Ruiz
Blandon
G. de Souza (sub A. Fernandez)
O. De la Cruz (sub K. Chala)
A. Aguinaga
A. Delgado
Result 4-0 Aguinaga, A. Delgado 2, K. Chala

243: 2nd April 1997
v PERU *Lima*
Ibarra
W. Rivera
A. Montano
I. Hurtado
L. Capurro (Sent Off 83)
Ruiz (sub K. Chala)
H. Carabali
Blandon
A. Aguinaga
A. Delgado (Sent Off 48)
Graziani (sub E. Hurtado)
Result 1-1 A. Aguinaga (pen)

244: 30th April 1997
v ARGENTINA *Buenos Aires*
Ibarra
W. Rivera (sub Urbano)
R. Noriega
A. Montano
Mendez
Blandon
H. Carabali
G. de Souza
K. Chala (sub O. De la Cruz)
A. Aguinaga
E. Hurtado
Result 1-2 A. Aguinaga